Mary J Moerbe is an LCMS Lutheran deaconess and author. She and her beloved husband, Rev. Ned A Moerbe, are blessed with six children, whom they homeschool. Mary encourages Lutheran readers and writers at maryjmoerbe.com and organizes free resources & a digital marketplace at LutheranHomeschool.com. Check out her other books on Amazon, including her children's books: *How Can I Help: God's Calling for Kids* and *Whisper, Whisper: Learning about Church*.

Jamie Truwe is married to her favorite Lutheran pastor and they, too, have been blessed with six children. Jamie is a small business owner at Pure Joy Creative and a part-time Lutheran school art teacher. She has illustrated margins for *The Enduring Word Bible*, along with crafting many other resources for church and home available at PureJoyCreative.com & PureJoyCreative on Etsy.

Naomi Truwe is the eldest daughter of Greg and Jamie (14 at the time of this project!). She writes novels and draws for commission in her free time. She loves theatre, music, and the arts.

Copyright © 2021 text by Mary J Moerbe
Copyright © 2021 illustrations by Jamie and Naomi Truwe

All rights reserved. No part of this book may be reproduced in any form without written permission, except in the case of brief quotations with citation.

ISBN 9781673704983

Published by MJM Publishing through KDP Direct Publishing

Glory to the Father, Son, Holy Spirit, Three in One!
Always One, yet always Three. Let's explore the mystery!

Almighty God says, "Worship me,"

And Jesus names Him 1-2-3.

Father, Holy Spirit, Son -

They tell us what our God has done!

The Trinity gave life and earth,

Then hope, salvation, and new birth.

The Bible shows God's Law and Grace.

God speaks His Word to the human race.

The Father gives us every gift.

He's mighty, strong, with mercy swift!

The Father sent His only Son.

God's Word-Made-Flesh salvation won!

The Word-Made-Flesh comes to us all:

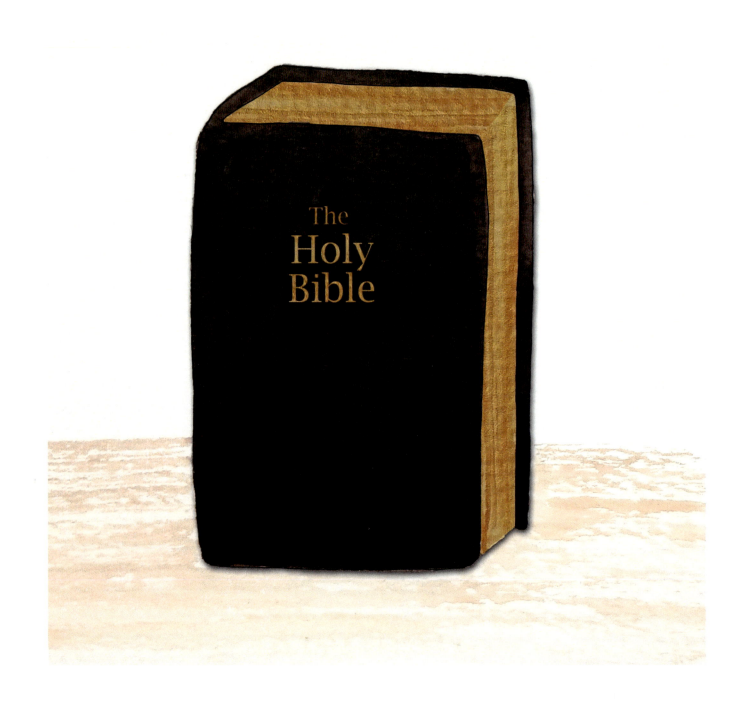

The Baby born in humble stall.

Jesus lived and died for me

That I may praise the Trinity!

The Spirit brings us God's own Word.

He gives us faith through what is heard.

One God gives us all we need:

His Son and Spirit, His Word and Deed.

We praise and worship God above.

Give thanks for mercy, salvation, and love.

Three-in-One and One-in-Three:

That's our God, the Trinity!

One God, though it's hard to explain

How Three talk together and share one Name.

Nothing is like Him! That is a fact!

Let's agree to leave it at that!

Creator, Redeemer and Spirit most holy,

We thank You and praise You and worship You only!

Glory to the Father, Son, Holy Spirit, Three in One!

Endorsements

"*Trinity for Tots* teaches with beauty and rhyme the great mystery of the Father, Son, and Holy Spirit. This wonderful book will delight parents and children alike."
- Rev. Dr. Carl Beckwith, author of *The Holy Trinity* (Confessional Lutheran Dogmatics Series, Volume 3, Luther Academy, 2016) and *Hilary of Poitiers on the Trinity* (Oxford University Press, 2008).

"This little book offers a wonderful, faithful, and simple definition of the Trinity that children can understand. The rhymes and artwork kept my children interested. The book provided several opportunities to stop and teach the children. Recommended!"
- Rev. Garen Pay, pastor, parent, and author.

"The mystery of the Trinity is a difficult concept for anyone to grasp. Mary Moerbe's inspired, eloquent poetry combined with the watercolor pictures leads readers to the inspirational message in *Trinity for Tots*."
- David Birnbaum, Principal of First Lutheran School & Education Executive of the LCMS Oklahoma District.

"A marriage of engaging illustrations and orthodox text, complimenting a liturgical lifestyle, *Trinity for Tots* is another winner by Deaconess Mary Moerbe! This title is the perfect addition to the Christian's arsenal of spiritual weapons against Satan's attacks, equipping parents with a tool to tackle this tricky topic with our most tender little ones."
- Marie MacPherson, classical educator, homeschool mother, and author of *Meditations on the Vocation of Motherhood* (Into Your Hands, LLC) and *Teaching Children Chastity for Life* (Lutherans for Life).

"The God of the Bible and of our salvation is Father, Son and Holy Spirit. There is no Christian faith other than in this God. Yet, as a deep mystery it is difficult to speak of him as one God in three Persons. For this very reason this book is priceless. It gives a primer on how to think and how to speak of Him as our Father who in his Son gives to us the Spirit of eternal life."
- Rev. Dr. William Weinrich, Professor of Early Church and Patristic Studies at Concordia Theological Seminary (Fort Wayne, Ind.).

"And the catholic faith is this, that we worship one God in Trinity and Trinity in Unity, neither confounding the persons nor dividing the substance" (Athanasian Creed, *Lutheran Service Book*, p. 319). And therein lies the great joy of this delightful little offering by Mary Moerbe. It introduces tots to the joy of this One in Three and Three in One whom we worship as catholic Christians. The genius of tots is that they believe what they are told without insisting on first having to understand HOW what they are told can be so. In this delightfully illustrated and simply written volume the mystery of the Holy Trinity is proclaimed, not explained, to children who are thus brought into His adoration and praise. And they can indeed WORSHIP Him even if (like the rest of us) they will never comprehend the infinite mystery of His being!"
-- Rev. William Weedon, pastor, author, host of *The Word Endures Forever*, and former Director of Worship and Chaplain for the Lutheran Church—Missouri Synod.

Made in the USA
Las Vegas, NV
08 January 2022